FREED INDEED
CHRISTIAN POETRY

FREED INDEED
CHRISTIAN POETRY

~~~~~~~~

The life and Rhymes of
Gary A. Rothhaar

To order additional copies of this book, contact:
Xlibris Corporation
1-888-795-4274
www.Xlibris.com
Orders@Xlibris.com
118568

TABLE OF CONTENTS

DEDICATION

I dedicate this publication to my Lord and Savior Jesus Christ for He is the one who forgave my sins, saved my soul, indwells me with the Holy Spirit, revealed His Word to me, and inspired the writings of these poems, and without Him I can do nothing.

FORWARD

My tenth grade English teacher's name was Mrs. DeMott. She had been teaching for many years and each year she would ask anyone in her new English class to voluntarily write a poem. It could be on any subject, any length, or any style. She remarked that there had never been a year when she did not receive at least one poem from each class.

She wasn't one of my favorite teachers because I thought she was kind of grouchy, but nevertheless I wrote a very simple poem for her. As it turned out, I was the only one who came through for her that year by volunteering a poem.

She really seemed to like the poem and told me how happy she was that I wrote it. The poem was this:

My Seaside Resort

I gazed from the window of my seaside home
And watched a wave come rolling in
So beautiful, so smooth, capped with white foam
But then it returned to the sea again

Oh well; I'll wait for the next

The next wave came and did the same
Its life was much too short
But now I learn they must take their turn
At greeting my seaside resort

That was the first time I had ever seen this women in a truly happy mood, and it made me think that my poetry could have a positive impact on people's lives. I found out later that she wasn't really a grouchy person at all. She was just a no nonsense teacher who believed in discipline for the betterment of the students. I have not been able to locate her but I hope that she is still alive and well because I would like to show her some my latest poems. I would love to make her happy one more time, and thank her for how she has influenced my life.

My next inspiration came as a result of company downsizing that suddenly forced many of my friends into retirement. I wanted these people to know how much we enjoyed working with them, and how much they would be missed.

I began to write customized poems that accurately illustrated character traits that were unique to each individual. I tried to make each poem humorous and complimentary. I always showed the poem to the person for whom it was written before posting it, or reading it at their retirement party, just to make sure that the content was okay with them.

Occasionally I wrote long poems that were usually based of true stories. They would contain strong messages that people can relate to, and possibly pick up a word or two of wisdom. Many of those poems would have surprise endings.

My pet peeve about modern poetry is that so much of it doesn't rhyme at all. I think they call it free verse or free style, but I think poetry should rhyme. If it doesn't rhyme, then it's perhaps some kind of literary art.

My final goal at my place of employment, just before I retire, is to write a very sincere "farewell poem" to my co-workers and tell them how much I have enjoyed working with them. After retirement, I hope to write more poetry and eventually publish a collection of poems that could have a positive impact of the lives of those who read them.

*   *   *   *

Well, guess what? I am now retired and the time has come for me to put this collection of poetry together and to publish it. I pray that it will be a blessing to every person who takes the time to read it.

Part 1
PREFACE

This publication is divided into two parts. The **first part** is a collection of longer and more meaningful poems. The **second part** is composed of a collection of short, light hearted poems written for friends who were retiring. Each poem in either part will be preceded by a brief explanation of the poem to follow. Please take a moment to read these brief explanations so as to better understand the story line of each poem.

WHERE TO BEGIN ?

Freed Indeed is the poem I have chosen to list first in this publication because it reflects my basic testimony; before and after I accepted Jesus Christ as my personal Savior. When my soul was hopelessly lost, He sought me, and saved me. He forgave me, and gave me the peace, joy, and assurance of eternal life. I shall be forever grateful to Him.

The poem, **"Freed Indeed"** is now etched permanently on the back of my tombstone so I can give glory to God for my salvation, even after my passing.

I was 32 years old when I asked Jesus to forgive my sins, and to come into my heart, and be the Lord of my life. I asked Him to help me understand the truth of His word, and the spirit of his love. It was the best decision I have ever made.

The years prior to my conversion were filled with doubt and confusion. I had no solid theological foundation, and my life seemed to be without rhyme or reason.

But Jesus said "be born again, my blood can wash away your sin and make you see the truth that frees, and sets your soul and mind at ease

John 8:36 Jesus said "If the Son shall make you free, ye shall be free indeed." The words of this poem are now engraved on the back of my tombstone.

Freed Indeed

What a waste of time and life

What a world of pain and strife

Knows the man who lives there in

Shackled by his load of sin

Himself he tries to justify

Admit his guilt; he'd rather die

Ignorant of a better way

He struggles on from day to day

He thinks that no one really cares

His hurting heart he never shares

But, what he does not understand

Is God has always had it planned

To rid our lives of that which binds
And free our hearts, and souls, and minds
To make his life a blessed one
Filled with peace, and hope, and fun

But then how can God make it be
This man is blind, and can not see

But Jesus said "be born again,
My blood can wash away your sin"
And make you see the truth that frees
And sets your soul and mind at ease

This gift of love he offered me
I am that foolish man you see

Though fearful of this "better way"
Accepted I that very day

My life goes on, but not the same
Forgiveness has replaced my shame
My spark of faith is now a flame
His book of life contains my name

The Holy Spirit lives now in me
And gives me joy abundantly
Grace and truth have set me free
To live with Christ eternally

Thank you Jesus

A Hard Price to Pay is a poem based on an actual incident that happened to the author when he was nine years old. Before environmental issues became a public concern , many small villages had what was called "the town's dump". It was usually located on the outer edge of a village. In this true story the author's father tended a strawberry patch near the site of the town's dump. The "longnecks" mentioned in this poem refer to discarded beer bottles.

A Hard Price to Pay

It happened many years ago when I was maybe nine

I had a cousin, name was Curt, we got along just fine

One day I heard my daddy say, "hey boys, come with me,

We're going to the strawberry patch, there something I want you to see"

He showed us how to till the soil, and how to plant the plants

He showed us how to strew the straw, and how to control the ants

We watched and listened for a while, our minds began to stray

Boys will be boys you know, we just wanted to play

We wandered to the edge of town

where trash was dumped right on the ground

Trash to others, was treasure to us

we couldn't wait to get into that stuff

Whatever we wanted we knew we could take

But then Curt shouted,"*watch out, there's a snake*"

Although it was large, it was moving quite slow

We picked up some *longnecks and started to throw

Curtis wound up, and then he let go

I raised up quickly , and took the full blow

6

The snake had no problem, it easily fled
Cause I blocked his shot with the back of my head
Semi-consciously stumbling around
It didn't take long for me to fall down

It seemed very likely that I was hurt bad
I knew that I had to get back to my dad
So lost and confused , no bearings I found
Each time I got up , I quickly fell down

Finally, wisely, I stayed on my knees
And looked for my father beyond the Oak trees
His image was blurry and hard to perceive
I figured I better just stay on my knees

Moment by moment his image grew clear
With each passing moment I'm feeling less fear
Now on a straight path I drew close to him
My situation seemed so much less grim

My fathers compassion for his injured boy
Turned all of my pain and fear into joy
He carried me home where he comforted me
He nursed me, and spoke to me so tenderly

He said," hear me son, I've something to say"
It's not that I don't want my children to play
But, when out on your own from your father you stray
There will always be "*a hard price to pay*"

This poem is based on a true story that occurred in the very small town of Carrothers, Ohio when the author was 12 years old. This poem was written about 45 years later.

A Stick and a Stone

I had a friend named Fredrick Brown

Fred lived on the south side of town

I lived on the north side, just one stone throw away

Yes, it was a tiny town, no stop light to display

Fredrick called me on the phone

He said "that he was all alone

Could I come there at half past six ?"

He wanted to show me a clever new trick

Okay Freddy, I'll be there

I'll have to walk, cause my bike needs repair

Tomorrow's my birthday, I'll be twelve then you know

I'm going to the fair with Uncle Bill and Aunt Flo

Well, Freddy's trick was really slick

He started with a three foot stick

At one end he cut a slit

Into which a small stone fit

Then he looked up to the sky

And hurled that stone a mile high

I stood amazed as I watched it go

And then he said "it's your turn to throw"

We threw stones for more than an hour

It seemed like we had supernatural power

I told my friend "I sure had fun throwing,

But now it was time for me to be going"

While walking home, I just had to do it

I found one more stone and straight up I threw it

But what goes up must come down

And then I heard a startling sound

Not sure what it was, I just kept on walking

But when I got home, my parents were talking

To people I know, Uncle Bill and Aunt Flo

They bought a new car which they came there to show

The car was so nice; I thought they'd be glad

But as I drew near I saw why they were mad

Their windshield was cracked as they drove into town

They suddenly heard a startling sound

I didn't "fess up", but I now wish I had

I forgot to consider the wisdom of dad

He knew about those sticks, and what they could do

"Were you throwing stones son"? I said, "Just a few"

The car was insured, but nevertheless,

My dad said, "No fair, cause you didn't confess"

Who was more shocked, I really don't know

Was it myself, Uncle Bill, or Aunt Flo ?

"No Fair", could he mean it ? We were all set to go

I meant no harm when I made that throw

Then daddy grinned and said "cheer up my son,

Tomorrow's your birthday, please go and have fun,

I have just one question to ask all of you.

When you go to the fair,... *could I please go to ?*"

This true story is based on a serious problem that occurred before the birth of my granddaughter. While in the womb she had a bowel movement, and ingested some stool into her lungs. When the umbilical cord was cut, she could not get enough oxygen, so they put her in an incubator and rushed her to a hospital in Toledo Ohio, then to Ann Arbor Mi. where she was put into a drug induced coma and given 100% oxygen until she could take regular air.

This unpleasant memory has served to draw our families even closer, and remind us how fragile and precious life is. "To God be the glory for answering prayers."

Emily Kay

Chris worked hard around the yard
To make their house look great
While inside his lovely bride
Put dinner on the plate

Their lakeside home was quite serene
Life was normal and routine
Expecting child at any time
Kathlene was calm and feeling fine

Until that blessed day in May
When on the scene came Emily Kay
Caesarian birth was the only way
Kathlene was sore, but doing okay

For Emily on the other hand
Things did not quite go as planned
The maternity ward had turned code blue
The call to action for a special crew

Chris was puzzled, wandering why
No one would tell him as they rushed by
Emily was struggling to breath you see
Her lungs were polluted with toxic debris

Emily was rushed to Toledo that day
But things got worse along the way
Kathlene though hurting said, "I must be there
Give me some wheels, the pain I can bear."

Although Toledo had given their best,
She was rushed to Ann Arbor to finish the rest

The high tech equipment and staff that are there
Assured mom and dad she would get the best care

Ronald McDonald stopped clowning around
And came to their aid for a place to bed down
A massive prayer chain was behind the scenes
Fasting and pleading, "God, please intervene"

All had been done that could possibly be
Will she get well; we must just wait and see
Her stats were improving, improving quite fast
The miracle we prayed for, was coming at last

The bottom line; she's now doing fine
At home with her mom and her dad
Our hands we shall raise as we offer up praise
To God who has made our hearts glad

Thank you Jesus

Regardless of how hard parents try, occasionally, a child will grow up with low self esteem. If they are not happy with whom they are, sometimes they will try to be someone they are not. The young adult in this story is unhappy with whom he is, but he is also unhappy with the phony image he has created for a cover for whom he is, and he thinks these are the only two choices available.

A wise grandparent informs him of a third choice, and that is to allow Jesus to be the Lord of his life, and to bring out the best in him. This hypothetical story is written from the young man's perspective.

Choices

One on one, and man to man I looked into the mirror

Trying to evaluate to me which one is dearer

The man I am, or the man I see; both choices I deem equally

So which one shall I try to be; the real me, or the me I see

People say I've got it all; wealthy, smart, and standing tall

My life is filled with accolades; my image says "I've got it made"

The real me is not so great, in fact he's down right reprobate

This image role I play so well may someday send me straight to hell

And that is why I fear to die, but I must end this sorrow

I will delay just one more day; I'll end it all tomorrow

This young man is so depress he is ready to commit suicide, but why does he need to postpone it until the next day? Here's why.

Grandpa's coming here today; in fact he said "he's on his way"

He always brings such joy with him; I'm sure he is my one true friend

And now he's coming to the door; my image mask I'll wear once more

Disguising my internal war; this is the one man I adore

Came he not with empty hands, a present he presented
Fresh cut flowers that he grew, so wonderfully scented
Of course he asked me how I was, I said "just fine and you?"
He said "who are you kidding son, your heart is broke in two"

Your eyes cannot disguise the pain, that's gnawing at your heart
Please tell me what the problem is, before you're torn apart

The wisdom of this gentle soul, caused me to drop my image role
Confessing all, I trusted him, and asked him for advice
One on one and man to man, he searched my very soul
He said "a double minded man must always pay a price"

You only see two choices son, perhaps there is a third
Let's not rely upon ourselves, let's look into God's word
He opened up the Bible, and then began to say
The very words of Jesus, "I am the only way"

"The only way to heaven but repentance must come first
The way to be forgiven, even if you've been the worst
Peace that passes understanding," he went on to say,
"Can be yours eternally with Jesus ….. Shall we pray ?"

He led me to the savior, with words I knew were true
The moment I accepted Christ, my life became brand new
My eyes of understanding are now open to his word
Returning to my wretched past, now somehow seems absurd

The joy of knowing Jesus gets better every day
Grandpa knew it all along, *Christ is the only way*

What can be better than a faithful friend? Two legged, or four legged they are precious.

I have a Jack Russell Terrier named Lady. She is my buddy, and she has a four legged friend named Buddy, two doors down. Buddy's four legged friend is a relative that looks a lot like him. I also have a loyal two legged best friend named Ruth for whom this poem was written.

Buddies

Yesterday when it was so muddy

Lady went out to play with her buddy

They romped, and they ran, and they acted so nutty

I was so glad that she had a buddy

In fact, her buddy's name is Buddy

He daily comes down to pile his putty

Buddy brings a buddy that looks a lot like Buddy

Together they're making my back yard look cruddy

I don't want to be an old fuddy-duddy

So, I let them continue to make my yard cruddy

They ran, and they played till they all three fell down

I cringed as I watched them roll on the ground

I wish I could say that they only got muddy

But it just so happened that they rolled in the putty

Because of my cat, Lady's shoulder was bloody

Now, all three buddies were muddy, and bloody, and full of putty

So, I chained Lady up, and I sprayed her down

Chunks of crud fell to the ground

One thing I learned as I cleaned up the mess

Buddies are precious and I must confess

I have a buddy who's faithful and true

Through the mud, and the crud, and all that we do

Life holds no promise that it will be fair

But, buddies like Ruth are extremely rare

Thank you Ruth

This hypothetical story came about when I was in the Army at Fort Knox Ky. There was a forest fire in a near by county that was exhausting the firefighters. So, they asked for voluntary weekend help from my Army base. As much as I wanted to help, I was unable to volunteer due to a scheduled operation at the base hospital. This poem reflects the thoughts of my imagination while in the recovery unit. Please don't miss the spiritual message contained in this story.

The Man on High

Adventure is the reason why

We gave this army life a try

When called upon to give our best

We always seemed to pass the test

But this time we were doomed to fail

T'was by God's grace we did prevail

Our Captain asked for volunteers, a special job to do

He needed men of courage, a very special crew

A forest fire is burning in the county to the west

The firemen are weary, and they need to get some rest

Relief is what they need from us, they need it very soon

For those who volunteer to help, we must be there by noon

We were there with time to spare; experience, we had none

The air was smoky, hot, and dry; it felt like an open oven

Fire was raging to our left, and also to the right

We would guard the middle, new fires we would fight

Suddenly the winds picked up, hot embers all around

Starting brand new fires, wherever they touched down

Planes and choppers overhead; retardants they were dropping

The wind swept flames across the ridge; it showed no sign of stopping

This fire is quickly becoming more and more dangerous. It is shaped like a horseshoe; One half mile to their right, left, and front, but the back seems to be wide open. These in-experienced volunteers think they can get out the open end whenever they need to. However, an alert pilot in a small plane was concerned about their safety. He sees that the open end of the horseshoe is closing faster than any of them can escape.

One small plane was watching us, it circled round and round

Then it dropped one object, from the cockpit to the ground

A manual for survival, which we had no time to read

But the note taped to the front of it, we were wise to heed

The fire will surround you soon; don't try to make it out
By the way that you came in, though it is the wider route

There is one way to safety, but you must not delay
A narrow pathway to the north, it is the only way

We saw no pathway to the north; a smoke screen blocked our view

But to the rear, that broader path, was tempting to pursue

In any case, one thing was sure, whatever we would do

We'd stay together as a team, and help each other through

Our Captain was a faithful man, whom we could trust and love

He said "what say ye gentlemen, let's trust the man above"

Without a word all heads and eyes were turning to the north

Our feet moved out in one accord, for all that we were worth

We ran a half a mile or so, the smoke began to take its toll

The stronger helped the weaker ones, by giving them a pull

We found what we were looking for, that very narrow corridor

The climb up hill was quite a chore, a task that no one could ignore

When we were safely on the top, we breathed a long hard sigh

Some men were so grateful, they couldn't help but cry

Recounting how things might have been, we looked up to the sky

With joyful hearts and lifted hands, we thanked the *"Man on High"*

A must win district play off basketball game that we thought we had won, until the referees declared otherwise. My friend in this true story, "Susie Bogner" is now an up standing citizen, and a pillar in the community.

Wallop

Let me tell you all a story about a friend of mine

At a basketball game, when the game was on the line

The score was just a point apart, a second left to go

Our best shooter shot the ball, from 30 feet or so

The ball went through the hoop all right, our side began to roar

But then the referees cried out, "he shot too late, no score"

Then the other side rose up, and shouted twice as loud

Both sides began to flood the floor, a very unruly crowd

The "refs" were trying very hard to make it to the "outs"

Bumping shoulders in the crowd, among the jeers and shouts

I watched my friend go through the crowd; her purse was in her hand

She packed a *"Wallop"* on the ref, and through the crowd she ran

That was many years ago; she's changed a lot since then

I asked her if she did recall, what she did way back when

She remembered striking him, of that there was no doubt

But she didn't try to hurt the guy, just straighten his head out

Unfortunately, some people still abbreviate Christmas with an X in place of Christ, (Xmas). This is very offensive to most Christians, because it seems to be an attempt to "X" Christ out of Christmas. This poem was written as a protest against the use of that abbreviation, and as a reminder of who is the Reason for the Season.

Keep in Christmas our Savior's Name

O'er two thousand years have past, since Jesus walked the earth

O'er two thousand Christmases, since our Savior's birth

While angels sing the wise men bring, their gifts of gold, and myrrh

To celebrate and commemorate the coming of His birth

Throughout His life He called all men

Invited them to enter in

To His kingdom that shall have no end

He prayed Father forgive them

Throughout His life no sins He made

Yet by a friend He was betrayed

So, on the cross our Christ did pray

His precious life was fading away

Though the world was filled with wretched men

He paid the price for every sin

So, keep in mind Christ bore our shame

And keep in Christmas our Savior's name

Pastor Dave and Dot Baynes were finally retiring after many years of faithful Christian Service, and moving out of the area to be closer to their relatives. As a congregation we had mixed emotions; happy for them, but sad to see them go. This poem was written to be read at their retirement party. We wish them the best of God's blessings.

Moving On

We thank God on each remembrance of you

Your ministry here has been faithful and true

Your friendship and kindness has been very real

You've served the Lord here with incredible zeal

You've run the good race, and fought the good fight

Not in your own strength, but in God's own might

We're not going to say that it's time now to rest

Although we all know that you've given your best

Some how resting just isn't your style

Unless perhaps it's just for a while

To be still and to know that God's in control

And He'll be there with you wherever you go

You're people of prayer if ever there was

Lightning rods for power from above

Faithful folks availing so much

While in God's presence and feeling His touch

Dot, you have been a pleasant surprise

Even sweeter than we had surmised

We love both of you and we'll miss you so much

We certainly hope that you'll please stay in touch

Dave, a finer man we've never known

Because your own horn, you have never blown

A herald for Christ, you were called out to be

"To God be the glory" you've preached faithfully

Thanks you Pastor Dave and Dot

Charles R. Fugate, nicknamed Big Chuck; not so much for his size but for his person. Chuck was a leader by example, and a follower of Jesus Christ. He was the caller for a square dance club that I had joined.

Unfortunately, at the time I joined the club, Chuck was terminally ill with cancer. Nevertheless, he stayed active in service to his beloved friends in the club until he was just too weak to continue.

His wife Barb was just as un-selfish as he was. We thank them both so very much. As it turned out I read this poem as part of the eulogy at Big Chuck's funeral.

The City that is Built Four Square

My first impression of Big Chuck was that he knows his stuff

Calling any square dance would have to be quite tough

But Chuck was not alone in this; his help mate shared the load

Working hard behind the scenes and smoothing out the road

Many others did their part to help the club succeed

Gladly volunteering wherever there's a need

The fun we've had through out the years was more than sheer delight

The moral values they've instilled has helped us do things right

They did the little extras, they didn't have to do

Bonding us together with a special kind of glue

Workshops, newsletters, special events and more

All these things were extras that we are grateful for

With nothing less than confidence, we followed Big Chuck's lead

The atmosphere he did create was quite unique indeed

When Chuck got sick we shared his pain, and prayed God's will be done

Bravely he kept on serving us, so we could have some fun

We thank you Chuck, we thank you Barb; we love you both so much

Your sacrificial service here was blessed by God's own touch

You've touched the lives of many souls while helping us have fun

That's why someday you'll hear Christ say "that was a job well done"

For now we bid farewell to Chuck, but when we meet up there

We'll be dancing on those streets of gold, in that city that is built four square

My only brother's name is John. I wrote this poem for his 60th birthday celebration. We grew up in the very small town of Carrothers, Ohio. This poem is based on memories that he and I hold near and dear.

Hey Bro !

Hey Bro, what do you know ?

About those memories long ago

Some were good and some were not

Some were not an awful lot

Like on our bikes when we would ride

Sometimes wreck and skin our hide

Like when you fell upon a reed

Impaled your throat and made it bleed

The time you tried to help mom sew

You pressed the pedal and made it go

Your little thumb got in the way

The needle came down and ruined your day

Verse 4 refers to a kidney stone the size of a garden pea. To remove it, they first had to remove one of bro's ribs.

You viced your finger in the door

It went shut, and you went sore

Even worse that kidney stone

To take that rock, they took a bone

Things got so much worse from there

We lost both sisters young and fair

Shortly after dad passed on

And now, our dear sweet mom is gone

But guess what Bro? It's not all bad

Sorry if I've made you sad

Although we've lost our dear sweet mother

One thing's for sure, we have our brother

Verse 7, refers to John's wife Faye. Faye is a multi-faceted person who lives her life for God.

And how about Faye, what a gal

Secretary, travel agent, wife, and pal

Bless her heart, she lives God's love

With strength and wisdom from above

And your three kids have turned out fine

They'd be the best, if it weren't for mine

Now once again I must regress

And put your memory to the test

Tell me Bro, do you recall

At Uncle Ted's barn when you took a fall

That time you swung upon a rope

You must have felt like quite a dope

You started in a lofty mow

Before the hay went through the cow

You gripped the rope and began to soar

But not high enough to miss the floor

For several days your "bod" was sore

And you said *"I will do that no more"*

You watched me hit my first home run

But guess what really made it fun

Not that we won the game by one

But that you said "good job, well done"

Verse 13 refers to the time we flew to a small island in an old beat up airplane that was on its last flight before it was permanently grounded. What's worse; a frightening rain and thunder storm began as soon as we took off. The fuselage leaked badly, and everyone got soaking wet.

Once we flew to Put-in-Bay

On Albatross Airlines to our dismay

A thunder storm caused all to pray

But we got free showers along the way

Time will simply not permit

To talk about the horseshoe pits

The 5 foot stilts, or the pitch and catch

We never could make Skippy fetch

And now I bring this to a close

I hope somehow this poem shows

I love you Bro, an awful lot

When I'm in need, you're "Johnny on the spot"

Our children think it's really neat

The "Carrothers Brothers" are hard to beat

Susie, was a country girl who usually wore a cowgirl hat and a vest. She loved to do round and square dancing. One time she lost her name plate at a square dance, but the caller was teasing her when he said "they found it in the men's room."

Susie loved all kinds of animals and "yes", she really did have a caged mountain lion in her back yard for a pet. *Susie* also did part time transportation work for the aged,

Susie

She looks like Annie Oakley, but she doesn't have a gun

Although she will not tell her age, I think she's fairly young

A very active lady who really loves to dance

She will do the rounds or squares when ever there's a chance

She has a thing for callers, and hugs them every time

She takes their pictures, autographs, and tells them they did fine

One time she lost her name plate, but when the caller said

"They found it in the men's room", her face got awfully red

She's not afraid of spiders, or bugs, or coons, or snakes

A mountain lion named "Lucky" was her pet, for heavens sakes

She also has dogs, cats, and birds; she talks to them each day

Sassy's kind of sassy, but Ben just wants to play

She loves to help the old and sick, she drives them here and there

They know, from her, they can depend on tender love and care

Whenever you see Susie, she will have a joyful grin

I think I might know why that is; it's because she's "born again"

This is a very unique song because of the yodeling, (which implies joy) but it is even more unique because of the message that it brings. The message is: Come to church where you will be welcomed. There are many good things happening there; such as worship, fellowship, Sunday school, communion, the joy of knowing Jesus, and the hope of eternal life. The belfry mentioned in this poem was popular in the 20ᵗʰ century churches. It was located between the roof and the steeple of the church and it was usually accessible from the balcony. It contained the bell or multiple bells that were used to call the congregation to worship on Sunday mornings.

Church Bells

Church bells are ringing

The choir is singing

Everybody's welcome, let's go, go, go

To the house of the Lord who saved my soul

Hi ,do, lady, Yay, do, lady, Yodel ,ledel, odel, de

Bring your family, and your friends, even your enemy

Church bells are ringing up in the belfry high *Yodel, odel, de, Yodel, odel, de*

My favorite place is Sunday School

We learned about the Golden Rule

We learned of God's amazing love, and how to serve Him best

Until we enter into rest

We'll thank Him for the blessings that He gives to us each day

For strength, and hope, and joy, and peace, and answers when we pray

Church bells are ringing up in the belfry high *Yodel, odel, de, Yodel, odel, de*

Pastor Jueckstock will be there

The four square gospel, he will share

He'll preach it right, he'll preach it strong, he will preach it loud, and long

But, he will never preach it wrong

He'll tell us of, the Savior's love, and how He bled and died

For sinners just like you and me, He was crucified

Church bells are ringing up in the belfry high *Yodel, odel, de, Yodel, odel, de*

We'll worship there in one accord

We'll praise our Savior and our Lord

The Holy Spirit will be there to teach us right from wrong

We'll praise in every hymn and song

Communion will be offered there, we'll share the bread and wine

Reminded of our Savior's love, His sacrifice divine

Church bells are ringing up in the belfry high *Yodel, odel, de, Yodel, odel, de*

The fellowship is *oh so sweet*

We'll worship at our Savior's feet

The joy of knowing Jesus gets better everyday

Jesus is the only way

He'll call us to His side someday when all our race is run

Then we'll hear our Savior say, "That was a job well done"

Church bells are ringing up in the belfry high *Yodel, odel, de, Yodel, odel, de,*

Yodel, odel, de

On June 18, 2009 my 36 year old son, Jason, was in a near fatal motorcycle accident. He was flown by helicopter to Grant hospital in Columbus, and put on life support for five days. As he lingered between life and death, I recalled this true story.

We were on vacation at Myrtle Beach. I was about 43 years old at that time, and as I waded out too far from the beach I got washed out to the ocean by a strong undercurrent. I can not swim at all, and I had no life preserver. Jason was the only one close enough to help me, so I cried out to him. He was ten years old at that time, but he saved me from certain drowning by hand paddling his floating inner-tube to my rescue.

After his accident in June of 2009, as he hovered between life and death, in the Intensive Care Unit, I prayerfully wrote this poem for him.

What you have done for me

How can I do for you my son, what you have done for me?

You saved my life when you were ten, and I was forty three

Vacation time at Myrtle Beach, a perfect day to swim

Atlantic Ocean calm and clear, inviting us "Come in"

Although I cannot swim a lick, I waded in up to my neck

And then began to realize, that I was in up to my eyes

Each time I tried to walk or swim, I'd end up going out, not in

The undertow was much too great; it seemed that it had sealed my fate

The only hope I had that day, was in this little lad

How could I ask this tender child, to come and save his dad?

But ask I did, and none too soon, he saved my life that day
But now it's he who's struggling, and I can only pray

My God, my son, he's dear to me, please heal him if you will
The doctors have done all they can, and yet he lingers still

His fate is in your hands alone, and in your sovereign will
And we'll accept your final call, and we will love you still

So, now we left him up to you, we know he's in good hands
Regardless of the outcome, there's purpose in your plans

We'll praise, and thank, and worship you, for what you're going to do
We'll watch you work you miracles, just like you always do

Your mercies are amazing Lord, you've been so good to me
My dear son's health, you will restore, and bless our family

Our faith we place in you alone, while resting in your grace
Someday you will explain it all, when we meet face to face

UPDATE:

Jason has recovered surprisingly well and God is still working miracles today. Jason is certainly one of them and we shall be forever grateful. ***Praise His Holy Name!***

Based on a true story, this near tragic event happened to the author when he was eleven years old. Because Gary is grateful for his health, his life, and God's protective hand, he felt a need to share this story.

The Perfect Time to Hit a Tree

There's a time to be born, and a time to die

A time to ask not, and a time to ask why

A time to hold, and a time to pee

And a perfect time to hit a tree

That time was many years ago, when I was just a lad

A fun filled day of hiking, with my brother and my dad

While hiking down a mountain trail, I felt the urge to pee

As they walked on ahead of me, I slipped behind a tree

By the time that I was done, I knew that I would have to run

To catch up with my dad and bro, now I'd really have to go

I sprinted down the mountain trail; gravity pushed me like a sail

Much faster than I meant to go, I could not stop, I could not slow

I passed them screaming, *"I can't stop, I don't know what to do"*

My brother yelled, *"You have to stop, there's a cliff ahead of you"*

Dad's quick thinking saved my life, he told me what to do

"Hit a tree, hit one now, the first one you come to"

I hit that tree; I hit it hard, and went out like a light

Suddenly that sunny day, was blacker than the night

When I came to, the sky was blue, birds chirping in the trees

I heard my father weeping; He said *"speak to me son, please"*

Thank you daddy, thank you bro, was all I could repeat

Thank you daddy, thank you bro, please help me to my feet

I shook it off, as people say, and walked with them along the way

Not far from there we had to stop, we came upon that sudden drop

The cliff was high and wide and deep, they saved me from that fatal leap

Each day is like a gift to me, thank God, dad thought about that tree

We turned and hiked back up the hill, and came back to that tree

The one that blocked my fatal fall, and gave new hope to me

Although I know God is the one, who saved my life through His dear Son

Into that tree I took a knife, and carved *"this tree once saved my life"*

This story is based on an actual incident that happened to the author when he was twelve years old. The barn mentioned in this poem was not a full sized barn but it was still high enough to be very dangerous. Fifty five years later Gary wrote this story in the form of a poem.

The Barn

Summer vacation, it's now time to play

And what better place than a barn full of hay

With my twelve year old cousin, Curt was his name

We entered the barn but it wasn't the same

The farmer had filled the barn full of hay

We figured it must have been done yesterday

At the peak of the barn there's a tunnel no doubt

We said to each other "Let's go check it out"

The light at the end of that tunnel I saw

Was beckoning me to do the low crawl

When I reached the barn's center and looked down from the top

The bales gave way and I started to drop

Falling head first from the peak of a barn

Should have set off my terror alarm

Oddly enough, I was not afraid

My peace with my maker was already made

But I did want to ask God to please tell me why
At my tender age He would allow me to die
I still longed to know Him and call Him my friend
And love Him and serve Him from now till the end

My rapid decent was now in His hands
God has His reasons, and God has His plans
I landed quite hard on my heels and my rear
On the bed of a combine; an antique John Deer

I felt it give as it cushioned my fall
I sat there amazed; I was not hurt at all
I'm thinking *"What happened, did God change his mind?*
I know that He's gentle, and loving, and kind

But did He produce a completely new plan
Cause it seemed like I lit in the palm of His hand"
The bales were still falling as Curt scurried down
Producing a mountain of hay all around

Curt said to me "Gary, this really looks bad"
You better leave now cause my dad will be mad
My terror alarm had finally turn on
I sprung to my feet and was instantly gone

The very next day in the town's only store
I'm feeling quite well, though my rear end was sore
Curt's father walked in, and stood by the door
As he looked down at me, I looked at the floor

I tried to scoot by him and be on my way

But as I squeezed by, he had something to say

He knew the whole story as told him by Curt

He just said, *"I'm glad that you didn't get hurt"*

*This poem was written in honor of my dear friend **Ruth,** who was kind enough to do whatever she could to lighten my burden during a particularly busy time in my life. I am forever grateful to her.*

Thank You so much Ruth!

THE YEAR OF THE SHOVEL

In the year of the shovel, when my work load was double

Having a helpmate was great

Our work list was long, so we had to be strong

Cause we sure had a lot on our plate

From drain cleaning, to pane cleaning

From stone hauling, to Phone calling

From mending my jeans, to making ice cream

We sure got a lot of work done

Sometimes it was hard working in my back yard

But, I'm sure she'll agree, we had fun

We agreed to fill my ditch, and then to fix her deck

We could have hired the whole thing done, but I said, "What the heck,

When we are finished, then we'll be through

So, *if you ditch me, I'll deck you"*

Give *Rufus* some paint, and a brush or two

And God only knows what she'll paint for you

A landscape, a portrait, or much, much more

If you ask her real nice, she might paint your floor

Euchre is her favorite game

Ping Pong is her best sport

She's not too bad at Tennis

She'll surprise you on the court

But her "light-hearted laughter" will calm your deepest fears

And if you're feeling down that day, she'll dry up all your tears

She lives her life for others, always giving to the max

Even making sure, that my doggie has her snacks

She loves bible studies, and also Sunday school

She always does her very best to live the *"Golden Rule"*

She never, ever worries, because God never fails

She knows God will take care of, all of the *details*

She achieved, the middle agers dream

By feeling the same as she did at 18

She's *"My Fair Lady"*, and I'm proud of this gal

I couldn't have asked for a more faithful pal

"The Shovel", was a memorable year

And I'm sure that we both had a ball

This year should be just as much fun

I call it *"The Year of the Chain Saw"*

This is a light-hearted poem about a time when I came into work and couldn't find my favorite chair. I was fortunate and blessed to have a job that I could do just as well standing up or sitting down. This particular day I had worked hard in the morning so when I came in to work on second shift, I really needed to sit down. But there was no chair. Fortunately, I chose to channel my aggravation into writing this poem.

My Favorite Chair

Oh where, Oh where is my favorite chair

It used to be right there

Who would dare to take my chair

If I find out , I hope I don't swear

I know I should share, even my chair

That would be only fair

But , since without asking , they've taken my chair

Frankly, I no longer care

I usually don't care if they've taken my chair

Cause sometimes I can find a spare

But I've looked here and there

And I can't find a spare

So, today I'm a Grizzly Bear

Gurrrrr !

Melinda is my niece who is now a corporate lawyer, but her first job was cleaning restrooms with a team of co-workers who loved her because of the way she treated them. Melinda always treated everyone as an equal. She was always friendly, kind, helpful, and truthful. She left an everlasting good impression on everyone she met.

Happy Birthday Melinda

Melinda my dear, be of good cheer

Your life has a long way to go

Being 30's not bad, but it is kind of sad

To think that your now half as old as your dad

You have made the grade

Your not an old maid

You've already got you a beau

Life can be great when you choose the right mate

And keep all your ducks in a row

I don't *mean* to be *mean* when I give you the brush

It's to help you remember that life can be tough

While using "this tool" at R.R.D.

You treated your co-workers all equally

They loved you, and wanted to be more like you

Helpful, friendly, kind, and true

So use this brush with pride now and then

Know where your going, and where you have been

Just keep on being as sweet as you are

You'll do great, and you'll go far

Today is your birthday; We hope it will be

As happy as happy can possibly be

We love you Melinda, please know that we do

This day is so special, but then so are you

Happy Birthday Mel !

My friend Ruth was doing some puppy sitting for her daughter's pet. Ruth had invited me over for dinner and cards. While we were playing cards I took my shoes off under the table. I didn't know that Rex "the puppy" was under the table chewing up my shoes. Ruth offered a humorous solution for this problem.

Rex the Wrecker

Once there was a puppy, who really loved to chew

He was so dog gone ornery; he didn't know what to do

Hidden neigh the table, where no one had a clue

He nibbled and he nipped, and he ripped on Gary's shoe

Ruth said, "I hate to tell you, but I think your shoe got Rex'ed

But then you won't believe, what Ruthie dreamed up next

A plan designed to fix my shoe, but not with staples, stitches, or glue

But when she thought the whole thing through,

She said, "This Band-Aid strip will do"

Pete is a naturally lovable person who truly lived his life for others. When Pete gets happy sometimes he will dance a jig. He's a sky diver, and a long distance runner. Each winter he joins the Polar Bear Society to raise money for sick children. We all enjoy his cartoon characters of his fellow workers, complete with humorous captions.

Pete Sperks

You have to admire a man like Pete; loved by all because he's just so sweet

He never says a word unless it's kind and true. He never passes by without a "howdy-do"

Caring about others comes naturally to Pete,

Cause when he makes them happy, he gets happy feet

Some folks say "he's just plain nuts"

Where in the world does he ever get the guts, to exit from an airplane at 20,000 feet.

Or run a 5 K race in the worst kind of heat

He gives his blood for others every time he can

Pete will do most anything to help his fellow man

He'll jump into a freezing lake if sick children are at stake

His cartoon characters make us smile and lighten our load, at least for a while

Pete enjoys drawing; he's best at drawing friends

"Reflect the love of Jesus" is the message that he sends

Pete is not a worrier; he won't speak doom or gloom

He has a simple philosophy; it's *"botta beam* and *botta boom"*

Part 2
ALL OF THE
REMAINING POEMS

All of the remaining poems are about people I have had the pleasure of working with for many years. They are all short, light-hearted poems that accurately illustrate character traits that were unique to each individual. I tried to make each poem humorous and complimentary. I always showed the poem to the person for whom it was written before posting it, or reading it at their retirement party, just to make sure that the content was acceptable to them.

A brief explanation will precede each poem so that the reader will better understand the person for whom it was written. Please take a moment to read the explanation so as to better understand the story line of the poem.

Some of the following poems will be signed with an unusual name: *"Guppy"*. *Guppy* is a nickname that my friends have been calling me for years.

Aimee was quitting our company to work for the post office. We teased her about going "postal", which in some circles means "berserk".

Aimee

Oh No, say it isn't so, are you really leaving, are you really going to go?

Now whom will we pick on, now whom will we tease?

Who could be more fun than you, and make us feel at ease?

Aimee–lessly we'll wander, missing you so much

Hoping and a praying, that you will stay in touch

If it's true that you love animals, you'll have to miss us some

Although we can act primitive, most of us have thumbs

You have great aspirations, and things you must achieve

But if you're going *"Postal", Please, Not before you leave* !

Pete was a man of faith and integrity. He was also a fine craftsman and somewhat of a perfectionist. We wish him well in his retirement years.

Neat Pete

Our man Pete is really neat

In case you didn't know

He dots his "i's" and crosses his "t's"

And keeps his ducks in a row

He does it once and checks it twice

Just to make sure that it will suffice

As hard as the pressroom is to please

Craftsmen like Pete can do it with ease

And now my friend there's time for to rest

We all know that you've given your best

Practice your golf at your own leisure

Never let time make you an old geezer

Stay faithful and true in all that you do

Your friends will be many, regrets will be few

Your friend *Guppy*

He was lovingly nicknamed "Mouse", because his face seemed to, kind of come to a point. Mouse saved the day for me shortly after I hired in to a large printing company. I accidentally got an ink knife stuck in the ink rollers while the press was running at full speed. The knife would have gone in and messed up the press but fortunately it was slipping on the greasy ink. Then Mouse came to my rescue.

"Inky" was our printing company's mascot. Inky was an imaginary little mouse that ran from department to department reporting on the latest activities for our monthly newsletter. Inky never passed by a break area without stopping to clean up the crumbs

"Mouse" Hafner

Mighty Mouse you saved the day

When my ink knife went quickly astray

Into the ink rollers is where it did stay

While the press was running full speed away

Not to fear, Mighty Mouse was near

When a friend is in trouble he is there on the double

He was brave and daring, not one bit afraid

He carefully reached in and pulled out that blade

Best wishes to you after all you've been through

We'll miss your friendly face

The ole "Mouser" is gone but his memory lives on

Not even "Inky" can take your place

The Ole *Gupster*

A much beloved college student who helped us out each summer

Ranae

This poem is to the tune of the Beverly Hillbillies

Let me tell you all a story bout a very sweet girl

Her hair is always in a bun, or straight, but never curled

She's liked by everybody cause she has a friendly smile

And she comes around to help us out each summer for a while

Temporarily that is

When she hammers on a keyboard she can keep up with the best

Except when she is on third shift and needs a little rest

When speaking of her boy friend who is somewhere far away

She always seems to have the nicest things to say

X's and O's that is

Julie was a very pleasant person to work with. She has a blouse for every season, and lives in a very nice log cabin.

Julie

This poem is to the tune of "the Beverly Hillbillies".

Let me tell you all a story bout a very precious jewel

She's a calm and gentile person cause her head is always cool

She's so quiet when she's working that we hardly know she's there

But she'll tell you bout her grand kids anytime or anywhere

Bragging rights, that is

We can always tell the season by the symbols on her blouse

They stacked the logs quite neatly at the place she calls her house

Jewel is not her first name but it certainly could be

If you want to know her first name you will have to add a ...lee

Jewel – lee, that is

Errol was a lovable guy who, unfortunately, didn't take very good care of his health.

Errol

Errol, I hate to criticize

But this should come as no surprise

You need a little exercise

Your health you must not compromise

Lay off the pies and the cakes and the shakes

And cover that cleavage for heaven sakes

Losing you once is hard enough

But losing you twice would be just too tough

It's great to know a man like you

Helpful, friendly, kind, and true

In everything you say and do

Your sterling character comes shining through

Your friend *Gary*

Jim was a very humble person who has a sciatic nerve problem in his leg. At work he walks with a cane. He is also a part time Baptist preacher.

Jim

Let me tell you all a story bout a very humble soul

He has a problem with his leg and moves a little slow

Regardless of his handicap he does his job quite well

His complaints are few and far between as anyone can tell

He will practice what he preaches and he lives the golden rule

Although he is soft spoken he will be nobodies fool

When you see him in the break room there's this book he loves to read

He says it is *"the good book"* and it covers all his needs

God bless you Jim

*A young entrepreneur who invented and marketed a very tasty barbeque sauce he calls "Daddy's Best". **Dane** is a big sports fan; He also loved hunting deer until he had a freak accident. He was riding a motorcycle when a deer ran out in front of him. He hit it and was badly injured. The good news is that he's okay now, or at least, **"he's more better now than he use to was"**, if you know what I mean.*

Dane

Let me tell you all a story bout a man with a plan

He wants to grow his business just as quickly as he can

People say his product is much better than the rest

At home his children say "their daddy is the best"

Now he follows Cleveland sports; he's a very loyal fan

He also likes Ohio State and watches when he can

He use to love to hunt for deer, back then he did it right

But the last time that he found a deer, he killed it with his bike

Sorry about your pain Dane

Carol was a printing plate checker, and a mylar (reader) by profession, but reading of all kinds was her insatiable hobby as well. **Carol just loves to read.**

Carol

Let me tell you all a story bout a gal who loves to read

Her appetite for info goes beyond the normal need

You may see her in the break room with her feet upon a chair

As she's flipping through the pages she don't seem to have a care

Mylars are her specialty she reads them like a pro

She also likes to read some plates as many people know

When she gets home she grabs her books and reads for several hours

I hope this rumor isn't true, she reads while taking showers

Give it a rest Carol

Clete was a light-hearted, outspoken, un-inhibited and fun guy to work with. We will miss his light hearted humor.

Clete

About Clete Franks what can we say?

A happy guy most every day

He makes his work seem just like play

His humor often makes your day

He's not too bashful, not too shy

A very outspoken kind of a guy

Out spoken or not

There's an empty spot

Where one of our own used to be

Stay happy my friend

This isn't the end

It's simply the way life should be

Best wishes Clete, *Guppy*

John is a bashful guy who asked me not to write a poem for him because he didn't want to be put on display if I posted it. After I wrote him this "note" he said I could post it.

John's best friend at work was a lady named Judy.

John

Since you won't let me write a poem for you

I guess this "note" will have to do

You've stayed the course, and now you're through

I hope that your regrets are few

Judy thinks you're really cool

She must be right cause we do too

Best wishes John, *Your friend, Gary*

Terry was a person who loved to cook and share food with her friends. She was a very good quality checker at work and a loyal Cleveland Indian's baseball fan.

Terry

This poem is to the tune of "the Beverly Hillbillies"

Let me tell you all a story bout a quality gal

She is quality minded as anyone can tell

She does a lot of checking so she knows what's going on

And she often saves the day when things are going wrong

Haywire, that is

She likes to cook and fry and bake and share food with her friends

When birthdays are occurring she will try to bring things in

She's a dedicated worker and she'll help you if she can

And she wants us all to know, that she's an Indian's fan

The tribe, that is

By most people's standards, Mike had a very good job. He sat at a computer each day in a very comfortable work environment, protected from the elements, but Mike wanted to be his own man, and do his own thing, and work with his hands.

*To the amazement of his friends, and co-workers, he resigned his long standing job to work in "**the great out doors.**"*

Mike

So you would rather work outside

Have a red neck and leathery hide

Bib overalls and heavy old boots

That's how your going to make the big loot

You'd rather feel the wind on your face

With a load on your back, while you work your own pace

Do *things* your own way, and be your own boss

And you *think* that's a gain, instead of a loss

Well let me tell *you* brother man

Maybe I've had *my* head in the sand

Cause what your saying ain't sounding too bad

You may be just starting a brand new fad

Best Wishes to you Mike

Richard was a very entertaining story teller. He looked like someone who is familiar to us all. Richard was a little bit pudgy and wore a white beard, wire rim glasses, and a red apron when he worked. He was a jolly ole soul indeed.

Richard

This poem is to the tune of "The Beverly Hillbillies"

Let me tell you all a story bout a story telling man

No one else can tell a story quite the way that this man can

He learned to tell his stories from his story telling dad

Cause he listened very carefully when he was just a lad

Boy that is

He's happy with a belly laugh or even just a smile

He makes us feel at home, at work, if only for a while

So guess who is this mystery man, I'll give you one more clue

When you think of Christmas season, he looks like you know who

Santa that is

A young athlete who attended Bluffton College, but each summer he worked with us shooting color bars on printing plates in a light frame.

Allen

This poem is to the tune of "The Beverly Hillbillies"

Let me tell you all a story bout a fine young man

He likes to play sports; I guess because he can

Whenever they're in season he will shoot a lot of hoops

But when he's shooting color bars, sometimes we hear an "oops".

Bluffton is the college where he plays football

When he says "he's there to win" he is bluffing not at all

Here's wishing you the very best, success should come to you

When you think of all your friends back here

Please know you've made a slew

Best wishes Allen

After working many years at R.R.Donnelley (A large printing company) my Ole Pal Al was still in good enough physical condition to play competitive tennis well into his 70's.

Al's faith in Jesus Christ was evident in everything he said and did.

Ole Pal Al

41 years at R.R.D.

It boggles the mind, how can it be ?

And that doesn't count the years of O.T.

If you add those in, it would be 53

You're as steady as a rock, every day, every year

Always trusting Jesus, the one you hold dear

He has blessed your life in so many ways

I know you will praise Him the rest of your days

For 41 years, you have held up quite well

We'll always remember our ole pal Al

Helpful, friendly, kind, and true

They just don't make'um any better than you

Your Ole Pal, *Guppy*

Debbie was a very good worker except when outside problems were bothering her; then things might go a little bit wrong at work, and we would hear an occasional shout of anguish. So, I dubbed her the queen of "Oh No".

Our friend Debbie had a very unusual sneeze. It was more like a very load shriek.

Debbie

The Queen of "Oh No" reigns supreme

Her mark of distinction;

An occasional scream

Oh no, not again, what's wrong with it now?

That's it, I've had it, I'm going to chow

a.k.a. Deb is Queen "Oh No" you know

Accept for her "Oh No's" she's really a pro

A multiple talented person is she

Especially when it comes to karaoke

What we all go through when she gets the flu

Is more than you can believe

Watch out, stand back, take cover;

I think she is going to....... *sneeze !!*

Ben was a kind and humble man of very high integrity. Ben was admired by everyone who knew him.

Ben

*This poem is to the tune of the song "**Ben**" from the movie "**Ben**"*

Ben, you do not need to work some more

You have found what you've been working for

Time to do what ere you will

Your dreams you can fulfill

With time left over still

Ben, please know you will be missed by us

Even while you leave us in your dust

Go and run and jump and play

Enjoy yourself each day

Before you fade away

Ben, a finer man we've never known

Because your own horn you have never blown

Keep on keeping on my friend

Stay faithful to the end

Be the Ben you've always been

Best wishes Ben

Betty was a loud but lovable lady who loved to celebrate birthdays.

Betty

This poem is written to the tune of "The Beverly Hillbillies"

Let me tell you all a story bout a very happy gal

She is loved by everybody cause she's everybody's pal

She knows not what is bashful cause she's never been that way

When she comes into the break room she has got a lot to say

With volume that is

She has a favorite melody she really loves to sing

But if you stand to close to her your ears may start to ring

The song is happy birthday and she'd love to sing to you

So, if it is your birthday you may want to catch the flu

Absent that is

Kendra was a friendly, helpful, neat, and orderly person. She was even tempered and nothing ever seemed to rattle her. She led by example and it was great to work with her.

Kendra Holmer

This poem was written to the tune of "The Beverly Hillbillies"

Let me tell you all a story bout a very bright girl

She can juggle many problems when this place is in a whirl

She maintains her poise and dignity when things are not the best

And she shows us what she's made of when we put her to the test

Quality, that is

Production is important and she does it very well

Without ignoring quality as we can clearly tell

We've come to know her as a friend to whom there is a bond

All this despite her handicap , she is a blue eyed blonde

Cute that is

Marv and Merv Wilhelm were identical twin brothers. I didn't know Merv very well but I worked with Marv for many years. Some people called him **Will** because his last name was Wilhelm. He always seemed to have the answer when everyone else was lost. We learned to depend on **Will** when things got out of hand. **Will's** motto was "Work hard, and Play hard".

Will

Let me tell you all story about a man named *Will*

If you ever have a problem he can surely fill your bill

He's the "go to" man of department O.M.P.

He's the man at the *helm* as you will clearly see

He loves his job and he really knows his stuff

He keeps things going when the going's getting tough

He always wears a smile on a very friendly face

And he lightens up our load in the old work place

He has an "other brother " with a simular name

Some, folks think that they even look the same

He spikes a volley ball with incredible pace

And when it comes to Euchre he can really trump your ace

*Over the years I have written many poems for my friends at work. I always tried to make them humorous and complimentary. From time to time, some of my friends would return the favor by writing a poem for me. The following is **one example.** I would like to sincerely thank these special friends for their kind efforts.*

A Man in Department O.M.P.

Come and listen to a story bout a man in O.M.P.

When he's finished making plates, he writes his poetry

He likes to write his rhyming words, and must have what it takes

Cause we all stop to read them when we're going to our breaks

It shouldn't take you long to figure whom this poems about

It should be very easy, and there can't be any doubt

He should get paid some extra cause he keeps us entertained

But thanks to old austerity, all wages stay the same

Thank you, my anonymous friend

After writing poems for many of my friends who were retiring, the time has finally come for me to retire. My goal has been to write a final farewell to my friends collectively.

Since we worked for a large printing company, it seemed appropriate to name this poem, "Good Impressions"

Good Impressions

How long I've waited for this day to speak to all my friends

To tell you how delightful knowing you has been

I've seen a lot of changes through out the course of years

Most have been exciting; a few were wrought with fears

We've worked together as a team to manage what we must

Moving on with confidence based on our common trust

Maintaining friendships on the job requires some concessions

To be successful at our trade we must make *"good impressions"*

The competition can be tough, but we've met every test

That's why our customers can say "we are the very best"

The people make the difference, but only if they care

Attitude is everything when common goals we share

Donnelley is the place to be when looking for security

And though it's never been stress free, there's been great opportunity

I thank the staff and management for being fair to me

Respect has been the binding thread on which we both agree

I thank my fellow workers of whom I've known so long

Each day when I come in to work, I feel like I belong

If there were bad memories, they must have slipped my mind

Cause when I add up everything you've treated me just fine

Now I bid farewell to you, I wish you all the best

Regardless of what else you do, there's one way to success

Keep God's word within your hearts, and practice it each day

He'll guide you through whatever you do, *He is the only way.*

Edwards Brothers Malloy
Thorofare, NJ USA
October 25, 2013